The History Farce Guide to Georgian Slang

By Ian Warner

Credits

The History Farce Guide to Georgian Slang:
©Kittiwake Classics 2012

ISBN: 978-1-4717-1111-4

Writing and Layout: Ian Warner

Artwork: Public Domain Period Art

Most of the Slang Terms Defined are "adapted" from the 1732 Canting Dictionary which has been transcribed online here:
http://www.fromoldbooks.org/NathanBailey-CantingDictionary/transcription.html

Dedication

To the people of the United States of America:

If you aren't careful a world worse than this will be yours!

Foreword

This book is a resource for understanding the language and culture of 18th Century England with a particular view to the understanding of the world of the **History Farce** Roleplaying Games.

As far as history is concerned, despite my qualifications in Classics and Archaeology, I consider myself a rank amateur. This is not an academic work this is an outline of the basics for the enjoyment of gamers and fans of the period's history.

The Dictionary section appeared in the original edition of **Tough Justice** though a minor error has been corrected and the text has been reformatted.

Also included is a bit more detail on the silly and sordid world of **History Farce** and its rather odd people.

This is not reading for the faint hearted and pulls no punches however I do hope that it serves to teach not only of our past but of the dark remnants of it that linger in our present.

Think I'm being silly? Just take a look at the political, social and religious conflicts across the English speaking world today and tell me the 18th Century is over!

Moralising politicians take on a wife and a mistress to prove they aren't the homosexuals they rail against.

Children die on the streets having been kicked out by abusive parents whilst the neo aristocracy discuss robbing the poor for even more money that will just sit moulding in a vault.

Worst of all horrific crimes of violence happen behind the doors of pristine suburban neighbourhoods but even the few who know of them are reluctant to interfere in the scared "family."

This dear reader is not just about an interesting era of study. It's about the study of humanity itself.

The Voice of the Past

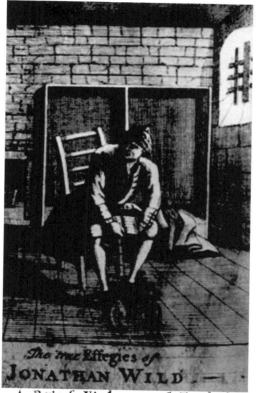

The true Effigies of
JONATHAN WILD

A Brief History of English Pronunciation

Speak Proper Like

Doing silly voices is part of the fun of
Roleplaying: Well it is for me anyway!

This Chapter is a brief history of how English
has been pronounced and written over the
centuries with particular emphasis on the
relevance of this to 18th Century Roleplaying.

This is based on my haphazard knowledge of
etymology and linguistics so if you know better
and want to be a smartarse do feel free to
contact me.

What do you get when you cross Celtic, Latin, German, Danish and French?

English…

Yes English is one of the most bastardised
languages on the planet. This is due to Britain's
somewhat interesting position as a resource rich
island on the edge of Western Europe. Before
the Norman Conquest of 1066 everyone who
was everyone on the mainland decided to go
over and slap the locals around a bit.

Eventually they settled and their language got absorbed into the ever expanding mess that was the local language.

The merging of these various languages was far from perfect creating a language that constantly contradicted itself in its grammar and pronunciation.

Old English Chaos

Different areas of the country had stronger attachments to specific incoming groups. As such dialects of Old English are almost diverse enough to be considered languages in their own right.

The administrators amongst the Norman nobility had quite a task in working out just what the Hell the regions were telling them sometimes.

What this emerging language needed was standardisation and when there is a need there is some shifty bugger ready to make a little money out of it!

William Caxton and the Triumph of Kent

William Caxton's triumph in bringing the printing press to England was also a triumph for his reason. The first region to print English became the region to determine the standard rules of at least written English.

The chaos was subsiding thanks to a remarkable invention that would finally give thousands of poor Monk Calligraphers a rest from their intense regime of writing out copies by hand.

Shakespeare's Tongue

Moving on to the Tudor era records become clearer as does the basis of our understanding of how people sounded.

Though there is still some debate as to exactly what the people of Elizabethan London sounded like the most likely theory is that they sounded very much like the folk of the West Country in Cornwall today.

That would explain why West Country actors are so much better and getting their tongues round Shakespeare's lines than even the classically trained masters of Received Pronunciation.

This was not the only accent in England by any means but it was by far the most common as London was the biggest population centre.

Class

For the most part Class didn't start to become a determining factor in how you spoke until sometime after the restoration. Most likely even legendary Kings like Henry VIII would have spoken in the appropriate regional accent (Lancashire in his case.)

As the nobility and common folk began to encounter one another more often the nobility begin to become aware that they are so similar and their worldview was such that they could not except that the lower orders were actual people: For their own consciences at least.

Thus we have the beginning of the development of the accent of the toffs Received Pronunciation.

This is a rather neutral tone with clear "clipped" enunciation.

The reason the voice sounds so silly and/or sinister was because the people who invented it were generally sinister and/or sinister. Think about that the next time you see a classically trained actor playing a villain!

Urbanisation

The final stage of the development of the English variety of accents, at least amongst the working classes, was industrialisation and by extension Urbanisation.

As machines were built to turn cottage industries to huge production lines people moved from isolated rural communities to various sprawling urban centres, some of which didn't even exist as chartered towns or villages before.

The working life in these cities was far faster paced and labour intensive than the quiet little rural existence that had preceded it. As such people began to speak faster.

As the environment got more toxic with smoke from the factories and overcrowding in the slums, people subconsciously avoided sniffing creating the somewhat distinctive nasal whine that defines a true Cockney accent.

Today's Accents

The result of this development is a wide variety of accents over the nation of England.

Whilst Wales, Ireland and Scotland have their own distinctive accents with a little variation in their regions many people overseas often mistake some English accents for accents from a completely different country.

From the fast speaking and nasal Cockney to the almost indecipherable Geordie (which is almost a separate language in its own right) there is far more to the English speaking English than Hollywood or any other overseas media ever highlights.

My best advice is to check out some examples in film and television. Preferably when they are played by people who know what the Hell they are doing.

Most of the time that means actors actually from that region: Even other English mean and women are shockingly ignorant of how other regions speak so your typical colonial actors don't have a snowball's chance in Hell.

Voicing Georgian England

The **History Farce** games have NEVER been about historical accuracy. Besides as we have no voice recordings anyone claiming historical accuracy in their faux Georgian speech is full of shit!

If your Roleplaying group wishes to get into playing around with silly voices, I highly recommend it, how shall they go about it?

By the mid to late 1700s the class divide is more or less fully in place linguistically. Some in the lower classes, particularly prostitutes and stage folk, were practiced at mimicking the clipped vowels of their betters but as a general rule if your Character isn't throwing money around like sweeties at a pantomime he or she probably speaks with some sort of common accent.

It is exceptionally unlikely that some of the urban accents, particularly Cockney or Scouser (London and Liverpool respectively) would have fully developed into what we know today but as I said historical accuracy can piss off.

Class divide is one of the central themes (if you go for that stuff) of the **History Farce** games and if you put on a voice emphasising this divide is far more important than any other advantageous bonus however fun it may be.

Regional rivalries can also be a lot of fun. I'll probably need a whole book to explain exactly why Scousers hate Geordies or Yorkshire folk don't trust people south of Sheffield so you'll need to put in a bit of research if you aren't familiar with them however there is plenty going on within the borders let alone when you bring the other distinctive nations of the British Isles into it.

There is an argument that putting voices on trivialises the Roleplaying experience. To an extent this is true. You could have a very serious group ruined by the one guy talking like Dick Vandyke but by the same token nothing is quite as intimidating as well done Scottish growl.

The trick is, as with everything in this hobby, to gel with the tone of everyone else and co-operate with your group to make everything fun even when your Characters are backstabbing each other.

Hell ESPECIALLY when your Characters are backstabbing each other!

The Slang Dictionary

The Vulgar Parlance of the Lower Orders

Georgian Slang

Particularly among the lower classes there was a tendency toward slang, shorthand and euphemism rather than saying things properly. Here are some examples of slang words and phrases of the time.

Repeats

Canting and Georgian Slang in general has a lot of words for the same thing. This was deliberate as particularly canny Thief Takers, Beadles and even Gentlemen started to learn Canting blowing its use as a secret tongue. Thus several words were used for the most incriminating of meanings.

Spelling

The 1737 Canting Dictionary from which most of these definitions originate predates the formalisation of English spelling. Thus words may be spelt differently from how we are used to them in a modern context.

Abram: Naked or scantily clad.

Adam Tiller: Decoy for a pick pocket. (Kudos to anyone who's completely innocent character is called Adam Tiller.)

Ambidexter: The practice of betting on both sides or in legal circles of taking fees from both defendant and plaintiff.

Anglers: Kind of thief who literally went fishing for goods with long hooked poles.

Assig: Short for assignation. Appointment or meeting.

Bacon: The prize of crime whatever that may be. Hence expression "save his bacon."

Badge: Branding mark.

Banbury: A tall tale used as a distraction.

Bandog: Bailiff or Sergeant at arms.

Barker: Basically the 18th Century equivalent of the commercial placard board wearers. They ran around outside shops drumming up business.

Barnacles: Shackles.

Baubee: Halfpenny.

Bawd: A brothel madam.

Bawdy Baskets: Peddlers of obscene literature and art.

Beak: A magistrate or Justice of the Peace to give them their full title.

Beard Splitter: A Pimp.

Beck: A Beadle.

Benish: Foolish.

Benefeakers: Counterfeiters.

Bilk: To cheat or deceive.

Bill: Sword.

Bingo: Gin or Brandy.

Bingo Boy: Alcoholic with a particular fondness for Gin.

Bingo Mort: Female brandy drinker.

Bit: Outwitted or drunk.

Black Box: Lawyer

Black Coat: Priest.

Black Guard: Shoe shine boys and girls.

Black Indies: Newcastle on account of the coal industry.

Blank: Looking guilty.

Bleating-Cheat: Sheep, possibly early rhyming slang.

Bleed: To part from money.

Blind: A feint.

Blind Ale House: The sort of establishment that doesn't ask stupid questions. Great for hiding from the law.

Block Houses: Prisons or other houses of correction.

Bloss: Shoplifter.

Blower: Mistress or prostitute for obvious reasons.

Blubber: Mouth or talking.

Bluffer: Inn Keeper.

Boarding School: New prison, workhouse or house of correction.

21

Bob Tail: Light woman, eunuch or impotent man.

Bog Landers: Racist term for the Irish.

Bob Trotters: Scott, northerner, highwayman or all three.

Boned: Arrested or otherwise screwed.

Booth: House.

Booty (to play): Throwing a contest. Deliberately losing for some reason.

Borde: A shilling. Half a Borde is sixpence.

Bracket Face: Ugly, homely or ill favoured.

Bravo: A hit man.

Brother of the Blade: Soldier or someone with formal sword training.

Brother of the Gusset: A Pimp.

Brother of the String: Player of a stringed instrument.

Brush: To run away.

Brusher: A very full glass of liquor.

Bub: Drink.

Bubber: Drinking bowl, heavy drinker or one who steals plate from public houses.

Bube: The pox i.e. syphilis.

Bubble: To cheat or deceive. Also used as a term for someone who is easily deceived or tricked.

Buck Fitches: Old lecherous fellows.

Buck's Face: A cuckold.

Budge: A budge is a house breaker who bluffs his way out.

To budge is to move sharpish.

Buff: A dog. To stand buff is to confess nothing.

Bugging: Bribing officers of the law.

Bulchin: Chubby boy.

Bull: Pimp.

Bull's Eye: A Crown or 5 Shilling Piece.

Bully: "Husband" of a Whore or Bawd or a wannabe Bravo who is in fact a total coward.

Bully Huff: Con artist who pretends to be a Bully or a regular Pimp and takes money off the punters.

Bully Cock: A Bravo who operates by forcing his target into a duel, acting as a second and rigging it.

Bully Ruffians: Highwaymen without any of the archetypal gentlemanly qualities.

Bully Trap: A cheat.

Bum: Bailiff or Sergeant.

Bundle Tail: Short fat woman.

Bung: Purse, pocket or fob.

Bung Nippers: Cutpurses. As purses went out of fashion this was reapplied to pick pockets in general.

Bunting Time: When the grass is long enough to hide couples having sex alfresco.

Buntlings: Petticoats.

Burnt: Carrier of an STD.

Burn the Ken:
Leaving an alehouse
without paying.

Burr: A dependant,
usually an annoying
one.

Butter: To cheat or
defraud by charm.
Origin of the
modern expression
to "butter up."

Butter Boxes:
Derogatory term for
Dutchmen.

Buttered Bun:
Having sex with a
woman who has just
had sex with
another man. Yeah
great imagery there
thanks!

Buttock: A
prostitute.

Buttock Broker: A
Bawd or
conventional
matchmaker.

Buttock and File:
Both a prostitute
and a pickpocket.

Buzzard: A fool
that is easily tricked.

By Blow: A bastard.

Cackle: To
discover.

Cackling Cheats:
Chickens.

Cackling Farts:
Eggs.

Calle: Coat or gown.

Cambridge Fortune: A woman of no substance.

Camesa: Shirt or shift.

Campaign Coat: Ragged coat worn by beggars to attract sympathy.

Canary Bird: Prison inmate: Origin of the term "doing bird" as in going to prison.

Cane Upon Able: Beating a man about the shoulders.

Cank: To refuse to confess.

Cannikin: The plague.

Cant: A hypocritical, two faced or exceptionally whiney person.

Canting: Slang of the criminal under classes.

Canting Crew: Beggars or Gypsies.

Cap: To swear an oath.

Captain Hackum: A fighting blustering Bully.

Captain Queernabs: A poorly dressed fellow.

Captain Sharp: Great cheat. I suspect Bernard Cornwell was making a joke with his protagonist's name here!

Caravan: A good round sum about a man also one who is cheated of it.

Carriers: Criminal message boys and couriers.

Carted Whore: Publically flogged and driven out of town.

Cash: Cheese.

Caster: Cloak.

Cat: Common prostitute. To "hang the bell around the cat's neck" is to attack first in a desperate undertaking.

Catch Fart: Foot boy.

Catching Harvest: Prime time for robbery.

Catch Poll: Officer of the law.

Catting: Using a prostitute to lure in a target or

prostitution in general.

Catmatch: When cheats or cheaters are engaged in combat with bad brawlers.

Cavaulting School: A brothel.

Caudge Paw'd: Left Handed.

Caw Handed: Clumsy and not particularly dextrous.

Chaf'd: Well beaten.

Chapt: Dry or thirsty.

Charactered: Branded as a punishment.

Chates: Gallows.

Chatts: Lice.

Chink: Money so called from the noise it makes in the pocket.

Chip: Child: origin of "chip off the old block."

Chirping Merry: Very pleasant when drunk.

Chittiface: A puny little child.

Chive: Knife, file or saw.

Chop: To change, barter or dispatch in haste.

Chouse: To cheat or trick.

Chub: Inexperienced gambler.

Chuck Farthing: Parish Clerk, so called because he was in charge of what little poor relief there was.

Clack: A woman's tongue.

Clank: Silver tankard.

Clanknapper: Thief specialising in silver tankards.

Clapperdogeon: A born and bred vagrant.

Claw'd Off: Lustily lashed or a carrier of an STD.

Clear: Very drunk.

Cleave: To make use of a prostitute.

Clench: A pun.

Cleyms: False sores self-inflicted by beggars.

Click: To snatch.

Clicker: Someone not trusted to share the spoils of a crime fairly.

Clicket: Biological term for foxes mating applied by some to human sexual relations.

Clinker: A crafty fellow.

Clinkers: Restraints in prisons.

Cloak Twitchers: People who steal cloaks from secluded dark spots.

Clod Hopper: Ploughman, often synonymous with stupid which isn't entirely fair.

Cloud: Tobacco. To raise a cloud is to smoke it.

Cloven: Victim of a female confidence trickster who claims to be selling her virginity but is not a virgin.

Clout: Handkerchief.

Cloy: To steal.

Cluck: A prostitute seducing a client into employing her.

Clunch: Awkward or unhandy fellow.

30

Cly: Money.

Coach Wheel: A Fore Coach Wheel is a Half Crown, a Hind Coach Wheel is a full Crown.

Cob: Irish dollar.

Cobble Colter: A turkey.

Cock Bawd: A pimp.

Cockish: Wanton, uppish or forward.

Cock Pimp: A supposed husband of a bawd.

Cock Robin: Soft easy fellow.

Cod: A good sum of money, a friend or a fool. Or I suppose a foolish friend with a good sum of money!

Cod's Head: Fool.

Cog: To cheat at dice. To Cog a Dinner is to talk one's way out of a dinner engagement.

Cogue: Small cup of brandy.

Cold Tea: Brandy.

Cole: Money.

College: Newgate prison.

Collegiates: Guards and prisoners of Newgate.

Collogue: To wheedle.

Colquarron: Neck, usually used in reference to hanging.

Colt: Inn keeper who lends a horse to a highwayman, Gentlemen Beggars or a Lad newly initiated into Roguery.

Colt Bowled: To be had by an amateur.

Colt Bowler: An amateur or inexperienced Rogue.

Come: To lend.

Commission: A shirt.

Common Garden Gout: Syphilis, also known as Convent Garden Gout as prostitution was rife in the area.

Comfortable Importance: A wife.

Confect: To counterfeit or forge.

Contre Temps: A fruitless attempt.

Convenient: A mistress or less commonly a prostitute.

Conveniency: A wife. Sounds about right to me!

Cony: Silly.

Cold Cook: Undertaker.

Cool Crape: Burial garments or shroud.

Cooler: Woman.

Cool Lady: Prostitute who sells brandy.

Cool Nantz: Brandy.

Cork Brain'd: Impudent, hardened and brazen faced fellow.

Costard: Head.

Cotton: Agree or understand.

Couch: To lie down.

Cove: A man who is usually roguish.

Covey of Whores: A well filled brothel.

Counterfeit Crank: A multi talented conman and forger.

Courtesan: A Middle or Upper Class Lady who works as a prostitute. They clearly don't think of themselves as prostitutes but that is what they are.

Court Holy Water: Fair speeches without action.

Court Tricks: Official state policy or political action.

Crack: A prostitute.

Cracker: The backside.

Cracking: Boasting.

Crackmans: Hedges.

Crag: Neck but can also be used for stomach or womb.

Cramp Rings: Bolts or shackles.

Cramp Words: Sentence of death.

Crash: To kill.

Crashing Cheats: Teeth.

Creeme: To pass something via sleight of hand.

Crimp (playing): Rigging contests for betting purposes.

Crinkums: Syphilis.

Crocker: A groat or a four pence.

Crop: Money.

Croppin: The tail or rear end of something.

Croppin Ken: A privy.

Cross Bite: To deceive a friend.

Crossbones: Nickname for a prostitutes and pauper's burial ground in Whitechapel.

Crown Office: To go to the Crown Office is to get drunk.

Cruisers: Beggars and Highway Spies.

Crusty Beau: Someone who blacks or masks his face at night: Itself a capital offence.

Cucumbers: Tailors.

Cuffin: A man.

Culp: Kick or blow.

Cull: A man whether roguish or not.

Cully: A Fop and a fool easily cheated.

Cunning Shaver: A sharp fellow who likes a close shave.

Cup Shot: Drunk.

Cup of the Creature: Strong liquor.

Curle: Clippings of money.

Cursitors: Lawyers on reduced circumstances who take on nigh on impossible cases thinking they can win.

Curtails: Type of shoplifter specialising in clothing and clothing material.

Curtail'd: Cut short or reduced.

Curtain Lecture: Women scolding their husbands behind the curtains.

Cut: To be drunk, to speak or to land a blow with a stick or cane.

Dab: Well versed in larceny. Origin of "dab hand" expression meaning good at.

Dace: Two pence.

Dag: Gun.

Damber: A Rascal.

Dancers: Stairs.

Dandyprat: Little puny fellow.

Darby: Ready money.

Darbies: Shackles.

Dark Cully: A married man who keeps a secret mistress.

Dawb: A bribe.

Dead Cargo: Disappointing Booty.

Dead Men: Empty pots or bottles on a table.

Dear Joyes: Irishmen.

Decus: A Crown or five shilling piece.

Degen: Sword.

Dells: Prostitutes just starting out by selling their virginity.

Devil Drawer: A sorry painter.

Deuseaville: The country.

Dews Wins: Two pence.

Diddle: Gin.

Dimber: Pretty.

Dimber Cove:
Pretty fellow.

Dimber Damber:
A crime lord.

Ding: To knock
down.

Dipt: Engaged or in
debt.

Dismal Ditty: A
psalm sung at the
gallows.

Dispatches: A
magistrate's warrant
to send a criminal to
prison.

Dive: To pick a
pocket.

Diver: Pickpocket.

Doash: Cloak.

Dock: To have sex.

Doctor: Weighted
dice.

Domerars: Beggars
who fake the loss of
a tongue.

Dose: Burglary.

Down Hills:
Weighted dice that
always roll low.

Doxy: A prostitute.

Drab: Prostitute or
outright slut.

Draw Latches:
House Breakers that
can only contend

38

with latches not locks.

Dripper: Venereal disease in general.

Dromedary: An incompetent thief.

Drop in his Eye: Almost drunk.

Drumbello: A dull heavy fellow.

Dry Bob: A witty or clever bit of repartee.

Dry Boots: A sly or cunning fellow.

Dub: A lock pick.

Dub the Gigger: Open a door.

Dubber: Someone proficient with lock picks.

Duce: Two pence.

Dudds: Goods usually stolen.

Dunaker: Stealer of cows.

Dup: To enter or open the door.

Dust: Money.

Dust it Away: Finish your drinks quick.

Eagle: Successful gambler.

Earnest: Share.

Easy: Manageable, normally this meant immobilising a victim physically but it could also mean using simple charms.

Ebb Water: Only a little money left in a pocket.

Edge: Daring for mischief. To edge is to egg on.

Elf: Little.

English Manufacture: Ale, beer or cider.

Equipt: Rich. Also used to describe how a particular victim paid for the thief's new gear. "The gentleman equipt me with this new coat."

Eriffs: Novice Rogues.

Eves: Hen roosts.

Ewe: Beautiful woman (yeah very flattering!)

Fag: To beat.

Faggot: To bind hand and foot.

Fair Roe Buck: A woman in the bloom of her beauty.

Famble Cheats: Gold rings or gloves.

Famblers: Sellers of counterfeit jewellery.

Fambles: Rings or hands.

Famgrasp: To agree to settle a difference.

Family of Love: Can be used to refer to prostitution as a whole but the word was taken on by an obscure cult.

Famms: Hands.

Farting Crackers: Breeches.

Fastener: A warrant.

Fat: Rich unlike modern Britain you never saw a fat poor person.

Faulkner: Tumbler, juggler or trickster.

Faytors: Fake Gypsy fortune tellers.

Feather Bed Lane: Bad road.

Fen: A brothel madam or prostitute.

Ferme: A hole.

Fermely Beggars: Beggars who don't fake sores.

Ferret: Corrupt pawnbroker or debt collector.

Ferreted: Cheated.

Fetch: A trick.

Fib: To beat.

Fiddle: A writ or to arrest.

File: To rob or cheat. A file is a Pickpocket who operates with a jostle and possibly a decoy.

Fire Ship: A prostitute with an STD.

Flam: A trick or false story.

Flanders Fortunes: Of little substance.

Flanders Pieces: Pictures that look good at a distance but don't hold up to close scrutiny.

Flap Dragon: An STD.

Flaw'd: Drunk.

Flesh Broker: A matchmaker or brothel madam.

Flibusters: West Indian Pirates.

Flicker: Drinking glass.

Flicking: To cut.

Florence: A prostitute in a dishevelled state.

Flush: Pocket full of money.

Flyers: Shoes.

Fob: Cheat or trick.

Fogus: Tobacco.

Footman's Mawn'd: Artificial horse wound used by beggars.

Footpads: Highwaymen without horses who use all manner of ingenious tricks to make up for this disadvantage.

Foreman of the Jury: On who diverts all talk to himself.

Fork: Pickpocket or the act of picking a pocket.

Forlorn Hope: Unlucky gamblers.

Fortune Hunters: Men who pursue wealthy women for marriage so they can take their fortune.

Foundling: A child dropped in the streets for the Parish to keep.

Foxed: Drunk.

Foyst: A cheat.

Fraters: Purveyors of false insurance policies.

Freeholder: Man whose wife accompanies him to the ale house.

Freeze: A cider used to dilute wines for sale.

French Gout: Syphilis.

Frenchified: Syphilitic.

Frigot Well Rigged: A woman who dresses well and has good manners.

Froe: Wife, mistress or prostitute interchangeably.

Frog Landers: Derogatory term for Dutchmen.

Frummagemm'd: Strangled or hanged.

Frump: A jest or witty remark.

Fuddle: Drink.

Fuddle Cap: Drunkard.

Fun: Particularly devious trick also backside.

Funk: Tobacco smoke.

Fur Men: Aldermen.

Fussocks: A fat woman usually used to refer to prostitutes.

Fustiluggs: A nasty beastly woman.

Gage: Pot or a pipe.

Game: Potential marks or, when in a brothel, prostitutes.

Gan: Mouth.

Gans: Lips.

Gaoler's Coach: A hurdle.

Garnish Money: Money spent among prisoners on first coming in.

Gelt: Money, some smart arse fantasy game writers actually named their currency this. Missing the point much!

George: A Half Crown piece.

Gig: Nose or woman's genitals. Also can be used to denote a woman of easy virtue.

Gigger: Door.

Gig'glers: Women of easy virtue.

Gill: A quartern of spirit or a homely woman.

Gill Flurt: A minx or a slut.

Gilt: A skilled lock picker.

Ginger Bread: Money, shortened to bread and still used in Liverpool.

Gingumbobs: Toys or useless baubles.

Ginny: Early form of crowbar.

Glaver: To flatter.

Glaze: Window.

Glazier: Housebreaker specialising in window entry.

Glaziers: Eyes.

Glib: A crime that goes smoothly.

Glim: Specially adapted lantern for Housebreaking. Also branding.

Glimflashy: Angry or impassioned.

Glimmer: Fire.

Glimmerer: Seller of fake fire insurance.

Glimsticks: Candlesticks.

Goaders:
Advertisers of
crooked gambling.

Goat: Lecherous or
lascivious person.

Gold Droppers:
Con artists.

Gold Finch:
Wealthy target.

Gold Finders:
Privy emptiers.

Goose: A fool or a
tailoring iron.

Goree: Money,
specifically gold.

Grafted:
Cuckolded.

Grass Widow: A
woman who
pretends to be a
widow but was
never married and
yet has children.

Garnnam: Corn.

Green Bag:
Lawyer.

Grig: A Farthing or
fellow.

Grinders: Teeth.

Gropers: The blind.

Ground Sweat: A
grave.

Grub Street News:
False news.

Grumbling of the Gizzard: Incoherent murmuring or rambling.

Grunter: A suckling pig.

Grunting Cheat: A pig.

Grunting Peck: Pork.

Gull: A cheat.

Gull Gropers: Bystander who lends money to gamblers.

Gun: To be in the Gun is to be drunk. A Gun is a lie.

Gundiguts: A wealthy fat man.

Gun Powder: An old woman.

Gut Foundered: Starving.

Gutling: Over eating.

Gut: A wealthy and obnoxious person.

Gutter Lane: The throat.

Gybe: Sealed pass.

Gypsies: I'm not going to go into the long and racist definition the Canting Dictionary presents. Suffice to say Gypsies are nomadic folk with associations with the occult and petty crime. Spending more than a month in their company is a capital offence.

Haberdasher of Nouns and Pronouns: Schoolmaster or usher.

Hacks: Hirelings.

Hackum: A fighter.

Halfbord: Sixpence.

Half a Hog: Sixpence.

Half an Ounce: Half a Crown.

Half Seas Over: Almost drunk.

Hams: Breeches.

Hamlet: A high ranking officer of the law.

Handy Blows: Fisticuffs.

Hang it Up: What's the score?

Hank: Advantage or coercive hold.

Hanktello: Silly fellow.

Hans en Kelder: Jack in the Box or child in the womb.

Hare: To have a swallowed a Hare is to have drunk dangerously to excess.

Harking: Whispers about borrowing money.

Harman: Officer of the law.

Harmans: The Stocks.

Harmanbeck: A Beadle.

Harridan: A brothel madam who is still working as a prostitute. Also used for shrew or noisy old woman.

Hartfordshire Kindness: Drinking to the same man a second time.

Hatchet Faced: Hard favoured or homely.

Hatches: Being under the Hatches means big trouble, usually prison.

Hearts Ease: Twenty shilling piece.

Heathen Philosopher: Particularly ragged fellow.

Heave: To rob.

Heave a Cough: To rob a house.

Heaver: The chest.

Hector: A coward with an inflated opinion of his martial prowess.

Hedge Bird: Sorry fellow.

Hedge Creeper: Thief specialising in searching or hiding in hedges.

Hedge Tavern: Ale House safe for criminal activity.

Hell Born Babe: Notorious youth.

Hell Cat: Lewd woman, still in use, sort of.

Hell Driver: Coachman.

Hell Hound: A lewd fellow.

Hempen Widow: Widow of a hanged man.

High Flyers: Bold, forward and adventurous women.

High Pads: Highwaymen.

High Shoon: Country clown.

Highte Tity: A romp or a rude girl.

High Tide: When a pocket is full of money.

Hob: Country fellow or clown.

Hobby: Named for Sir Posthumus Hobby: A lovable eccentric.

Hocus: Drunk.

Hog: Shilling.

Hookt: Tricked.

Hop Merchant: Master of dancing.

Horn Mad: Angry at being cuckolded.

Hued: Severely flogged.

Huff: Bullying fellow.

Hulver Head: Silly or foolish fellow.

Hum Box: Pulpit.

Hum Cap: Very strong beer.

Humpty Dumpty: Ale boiled with brandy.

Hums: Congregation at a Church.

Hunting: Drawing others into crime.

Hush'd: Murdered.

Hush Money:
Money spent to
conceal evidence.

Husky Lour:
Guinea.

Ill Fortune: A
Ninepence.

Impost Taker: One
who lends to
gamblers at
extortionate rates.

Inching In:
Encroaching upon.

Inlayed:
Comfortable in his
wealth.

Irish Toyles:
Thieves who sell
pins and laces as a
cover.

Iron Doublet: A
prison.

Itch Land:
Scotland.

Jack: A farthing. In
modern parlance it
has come to mean a
negligible value.

**Jack Adams
Parish:**
Clerkenwell.

Jack in the Box: A
con artist.

Jack Sprat: A
dwarf.

Jack at a Pinch: A
poor Parson from
Hackney.

Jacobites: Cheats: Named for the supporters of the exiled Stuart dynasty.

Jague: A ditch.

Janizaries: Has a variety of uses from prostitutes, officers of the law and various criminal gangs. Very confusing!

Jarke: A seal.

Jarke Men: Forgers of licenses and passes.

Jem: A gold ring. A Rum Jem is a diamond ring.

Jenny: Early crowbar.

Jet: A lawyer.

Autem Jet: A parson.

Jew: It's very Anti-Semitic but a very good trickster was sometimes called a Jew. Treating someone like a Jew was to treat them poorly. Not so much Anti-Semitic as an ironic reference to the Anti-Semitism of the time.

Jews: The Brokers Behind St Clements Church London.

Jig: A trick or a dance.

Jinglers: Horse racing promoters visiting country fairs.

Jobe: Guinea.

Jock: To have sex with a woman.

Juckum Gage: Chamber pot.

Jordain: Great crime, staff or chamber pot.

Joseph: A coat.

Juckrum: Licence.

Jumble Gut Lane: A very bad road.

Justice: To "do justice" is to turn King's Evidence and rat out your colleagues.

Kate: A woman proficient at picking locks.

Keel Bullies: Men who carry coal to and from ships: Derogatory.

Keeping Cully: A man who keeps a mistress with a very favourable financial settlement.

Keffal: Horse.

Kelter: To be out of Kelter is to be out of place.

Ken: House.

Ken Miller: House breaker.

Kick: Sixpence.

Kick'd: Fled.

Kicks: Breeches.

Kidlays: Con artists who divert courier boys and disappear with their parcels.

Kill Devil: Rum.

Kimbaw: To cheat or beat severely.

Kin: A fellow thief.

Kinchin: Little child.

Kinchin Coves: Orphaned or runaway Children inducted into the world of crime.

King's Head Inn: Newgate Prison.

King's Pictures: Money.

Kit: A dancing master.

Knack Shop: A Toy Shop with pretty devices to pick pockets.

Knave in Grain: First rate.

Knight of the Blade: A man with

56

pretentions to be a hit man or a pimp.

Knight of the Post: A mercenary swearer of oaths.

Knight of the Road: Notorious and well equipped Highwayman.

Knock Down: Strong ale or beer.

Knot: A gang of villains.

Lac'd Mutton: A woman, charming.

Lacing: A beating.

Lady: A woman with some form of physical deformity.

Lady Birds: Lewd women.

Lag: Water or last. In the latter case it became "lag behind."

Lamb Skin Men: Judges.

Land Lopers: Or Landlubbers beggars and thieves in the countryside. Nautical men refer to all non-nautical folk as such.

Land Pyrates: Highwaymen and other armed robbers.

Lantern Jaw'd: Thin faced man.

Lap: Porridge, butter milk or whey.

Lare Over: Watch what you're saying. Usually means speak in heavy canting so the officers/ gentry don't have any idea what you're talking about.

Latch: Let in.

Lay'd Up in Lavender: Pawned to settle a debt.

Leather Head: Thick skulled or heavy headed.

Leathern Convenience: A coach.

Let's Buy a Brush: Run for it!

Levite: Priest or parson.

Lib: To have sex.

Libbege: A bed.

Libkin: Lodgings.

Lickt: Made up.

Lifter: A crutch.

Lig: To have sex.

Light Frigate: A prostitute who also works as a highway spy.

Lilly White: Chimney sweep,

yeah great joke there!

Line of the old Author: Dram of brandy.

Linnen Armorers: Tailors.

Little Barbary: Yet another term for sex!

Loap'd: Ran.

Lob Cock: A stupid heavy.

Lob's Pound: Jail.

Lobster: A soldier: Named for their red uniforms.

Lock All Fast: Seller of stolen goods.

Lock (The): Store of stolen goods.

Lockram Jaw'd: Lean, sharp faced.

Lodge: Watch.

Long Meg: Unusually tall woman.

Long Shanks: Long legged.

Looking Glass: Chamber pot.

Loon Slate: 13 Pence and a Half Penny.

Lord: Deformed man.

Lour: Money.

Louse Land: Scotland: Obviously derogatory.

Louse Trap: Comb.

Low Pad: A Foot Pad.

Low Tide: An empty pocket.

Lud's Bulwark: Ludgate prison.

Luggs: Ears. Still used today in some areas.

Lullaby Cheat: A child.

Lumb: Too much.

Lurched: Beaten in gambling game.

Lurries: Small items that can be easily pilfered.

Macaroni: A foppish young man, named for certain club's delight in foreign cuisine. Could also be used to denote a homosexual or bisexual.

Mackarel: A brothel madam.

Mackarel Back: Unusually tall man.

Madam Van: A prostitute.

Made: Stolen.

Mad Tom: Lunatic or beggar pretending to be one.

Maiden Sessions: Court sessions where no one is sentenced to death.

Make: Half Penny. To Make is to steal as above.

Malkintrash: Dressed in a shocking state.

Malmsey Nose: Red nose from drinking too much.

Man o' t' Town: Debauchee or lewd man.

Margery Prater: A hen.

Marinated: Transported.

Marriage Music: Children's cries.

Masons Mawn'd: A sham sore designed to replicate a scaffold fall.

Maul'd: Very drunk or badly beaten.

Maunders: Beggars.

Maundring Broth: Scolding.

Mawdlin: Sad drunk.

Meggs: Guineas.

Melt: To spend.

Milch Kine: Attempting to bribe a prison warden.

Mill: To steal, rob or kill.

Mill Ken: Housebreaker.

Mill the Glaze: To break a window.

Miller: Killer or murderer.

Mint: Gold.

Mish: Shirt, smock or sheet.

Mish Topper: A coat or petticoat.

Miss: Another word for Courtesan. Bit of a misnomer as most of the famous Courtesans were in fact married women or widows.

Moabites: A group of officers of the law.

Mob: Prostitute or group of such.

Mongrel: Annoying hanger on in a criminal gang.

Molly House: A secret club for the homosexual community. Molly Houses provided refuge for this persecuted minority as well as a female manageress who pretended to be a fiancée of any member accused of the capital crime of sodomy.

Mopsie: A homely woman.

Mopus: Half Penny or Farthing.

Morglag: Watchman's sword.

Morris: To be hanged.

Morts: Yeoman's daughter. Also used in the possessive for one's wife, mistress or prostitute.

Mother: A brothel madam.

Mother Midnight: A brothel madam with midwifery skills.

Moveables: Easily stolen and concealed small items.

Mouse Trap: Marriage.

Mower: Cow.

Mow Heater: A drover.

Muck: Money or wealth in general.

Muffling Cheat: A napkin.

Mum Glass: The London Fire Memorial.

Mumper: A beggar who pretends to be a gentleman or woman in distress.

Munns: Face.

Mutton Monger: A sheep stealer or ladies' man.

Mutton in Long Coats: Women, again charming.

Muzzle: Unkempt beard.

Myrmidons: Watchmen and assistants to the Constable or Beadle.

Nab: Hat, to be nabbed is to be arrested which is still in use today.

Nab Girder: A bridle.

Nan: A domestic servant, usually a maid.

Nanny House: A brothel.

Nap: Cheating at dice, carrying a

venereal disease and the sense we know today a short sleep.

Napper: Thief or con man.

Napper of Naps: A sheep thief.

Nappy Ale: Very strong ale.

Nask: A prison.

Natural: A mistress or prostitute.

Nazie: Drunken.

Nettled: Teased or provoked.

Nig: Money clippings.

Nigging: Clipping coins.

Niggling: To accompany a woman.

Nigit: An idiot.

Nigmenog: A complete idiot.

Nikin: A mistress or prostitute with a particularly soft complexion.

Nim: To steal.

Nim Gimmer: A medical professional. Particularly one that specialises in venereal disease.

Nob: Head: how this degenerated to mean penis in modern vulgar parlance I have no idea.

Nocky: A stupid man.

Noddle: The head.

Noddy: A beggar who plays stupid and a card game.

Noozed: Hanged or worse married.

Nose Gent: A female hermit or recluse. Alternatively a nun.

Nub: The neck and the act of sex.

Nubbing: Hanging.

Nubbing Cheat: The gallows.

Nubbing Cove: The hangman.

Nug: Term of endearment that has fortunately passed out of use!

Nut Crackers: The Pillory.

Oak: Wealthy and respected man.

Ogles: Eyes.

Old Dog At It: Good at it.

Old Dog at Common Prayer: Poor Hackney Parson. Well-read but a poor preacher.

Old Harry: Concoction used to corrupt wines.

Old Mr Gory: A piece of gold.

Old Rodger: The devil.

Old Toast: An old man who is still light on his feet.

Oliver's Skull: Chamber pot. I think the Oliver this is referring to is Cromwell but I can't be sure.

One in Ten: A Parson (derogatory.)

One of my Cousins: A prostitute. This term is still used in American prostitution.

Oyl of Barley: Drink.

Ox House: Marriage.

Pad: The Highway or a Highway robber.

Paddington Fair: An execution at Tyburn.

Palliards: Second generation beggars who also beg.

Panam: Bread.

Panter: A heart.

Pantler: A butler.

Papler: Porridge.

Pairings: Money clippings.

Patri Coves: Conductors of unofficial and unchristian weddings. Also can be used to refer to real Priests particularly corrupt ones.

Peak: Lace.

Peculiar: A mistress.

Ped: A basket.

Peepers: A looking glass, also eyes.

Peery: Shy or nervous.

Peg Trantums: Dead.

Pelting Village: An obscure village or one that is good for hiding out in.

Penance Board: A pillory.

Penthouse Nub: Broad brimmed hat.

Peppered Off:
Carrier of an STD.

Petticoat Pensioner: A heavy involved in gambling. Usually ex-military.

Pharaoh: A very strong distilled malt drink.

Phenix Men: Sellers of false fire insurance.

Philistines: Officers of the law, drunks or drunk officers of the law.

Picking: Petty theft.

Pickaroon: Shabby pauper.

Pickled: Badly affected by Syphilis.

Pig: Sixpence.

Pike: To flee with extreme haste.

Pink'd: Wounded in a formal duel with swords.

Pit: Makeshift grave for gallows victims who cannot afford to pay for a Christian burial.

Pit a Pat: Really scared.

Plaister of Hot Guts: Huddling together for warmth.

Plate Fleet Coes in:
When money comes
to hand.

Paltter Faces Jade:
Woman with an
average looking
face.

Play it Off: To
deliberately lose, to
lose at gambling
and to cheat.

Pluck The Ribbon:
Ring the bell at a
Tavern.

Plyer: Crutch or
trader.

Poker: A sword.

Pops: Pistols or the
sound they make
when fired.

Porker: Sword.

Pot Valliant:
Drunk.

Poulain: A bubo.
Plague was dying
out during the
Bloody Code but
there were still a
couple of cases here
and there.

Powdering Tub: A
venereal disease
hospital in
Kingsland near
London.

Poisoned: Heavily
pregnant.

Poison Pate:
Ginger.

Prancer: Horse.

70

Prancer's Nab:
Horse's head, used
in false seals.

Pratts: Thighs,
buttocks or a tinder
box.

Prey: Money.

Prick Louse: A
Tailor.

Priest Linked:
Married.

Prig: A thief or a
nice idiot.

Prigging: Having
sex with a woman.

Prigstar: Love
rival.

Priggish: Thieving.

Prig Napper: Horse
Thief or Thief
Taker.

Princock: A pert
forward fellow.

Prinking: Dressing
your best.

**Mistress Princum
Prancium:** A
woman who is stiff,
over nice and
precise at the same
time.

Prog: Meat.

Punch Houses:
Brothels.

Punk: A diminutive
prostitute.

71

Pupil Mongers:
University lecturers.

Pure: A mistress.

Purest Pure: A
particularly loved or
beautiful mistress.

Pushing School:
Fencing school or
brothel.

Quail Pipe: A
woman's tongue.

Quarron: Body.

Quean: Prostitute
or downright slut.

Queere: Roguish or
untrustworthy.

Queere Birds:
Habitual criminals.

Queere Bluffer:
Sneaking, conning
or a cut throat
innkeeper.

Queere Bung:
Empty purse.

Queere Clout: A
handkerchief that
isn't worth much.

Queere Cole:
Counterfeit or
clipped money.

Queere Cussin: A
magistrate.

Queere Degen: An
iron, steel or brass
hilted sword.

Queere Diver:
Incompetent
pickpocket.

Queere Doxy:
Poorly dressed
prostitute.

Queere Duke:
Gentleman on hard
times also a very
thin man.

Queere Fun:
Messing up a con.

Queere Ken: A
prison.

Queere Kicks:
Tattered breeches.

Queere Mort: A
nasty slut.

Queere Topping:
Poor headdress.

Quibble: To trifle
or pun.

Quod: Can be used
to mean Newgate
but more commonly
refers to debtor's
prison.

Rabbet Suckers:
Corrupt
pawnbrokers.

Rag: Farthing.

Rag Water:
Specially purified
water.

Ranging: Male
promiscuity.

Rank Rider:
Highwayman or
jockey.

Rantipole: A rude
or feral child.

Raree Show Men: Pedlars of portable puppet shows. The "Professors" and their Punch and Judy shows are just about starting around this time.

Rat: A drunk arrested by the authorities.

Rattler: Coach.

Rattling Cove: Coachman.

Rattling Mumpers: Those who chase down coaches.

Rattle: Flee.

Recruits: Money.

Red Fustian: Claret or red port.

Red Letter Man: A Catholic.

Red Rag: A tongue.

Rhino: Money for services rendered.

Ribbin: Money.

Rich Face: Red faced.

Ridg Cully: Goldsmith.

Rig: Gambling game, diversion or ridicule.

Rigging: Clothing, to unrig is to strip.

Ring: Money stolen by Highwaymen.

Robberds Men: Legendary thieves.

Rochester Portion: Two torn smocks.

Roger: A Thief Taker.

Romer: Drinking glass.

Rook: To cheat a cheat.

Rosy Gills: Fresh faced.

Rotan: Vehicle or specifically a cart.

Rot Gut: Thin Beer.

Rovers: Pirates or Gypsies.

Rough: To sleep in one's day clothes.

Rub: To run or to live well.

Rubs to The Whit: Sends to Newgate.

Ruffin: The Devil.

Rufflers: Opportunist criminals who disguise themselves as war veterans (or are war veterans.)

Ruffmans: Woods or bushes.

Rum: Exceptionally good.

Rum Beck: Magistrate.

Rum Bite: Clever con.

Rum Blower: Particularly fine mistress of one man.

Rum Bluffer: A jolly Inn Keeper.

Rumbo: Prison.

Rum Bob: Good apprentice, neat trick or short wig.

Rum Boozing Welts: Grapes.

Rumly: With courage or ingenuity.

Rum Cull: Easily conned person or a man who is very good to his mistress.

Rum Dell/Doxy: A middle to upper class prostitute.

Rum Dukes: Handsome men or bailiffs.

Rum Duchess: Beautiful woman.

Rum Mort: Deformed woman.

Rump and Kidney Men: Musicians who live primarily off the scraps of the feasts they play at.

Rum Quidds: Great booty or large snack.

Rum Squeeze: Lots of wine or good wine.

Rum Ville: London.

Running Stationers: Street corner newspaper, book or pamphlet sellers.

Rustyguts: Old blunt fellow.

Sack: Pocket or to be drunk.

Salamon: The "sacred" oath of beggars.

School of Venus: A brothel.

Sconce: A level of trust.

Scoure: To wear.

Scouwre: To flee.

Scouwrers: The drunk and disorderly.

Screw: A common prostitute.

Sealer: A kind of street Lawyer who sells bonds and civil judgements. They weren't exactly professional but they were all that most people could afford.

Secret: To be let into the Secret is to be introduced to gambling.

Seraglio: A brothel, derived from the Turkish.

Seraglietto: A notoriously low class brothel.

Setters: Officers of the law or customs.

Settle: To knock out.

Shappeau: Hat, from the military shako and the French Chapeau.

Sharper: A con man.

Sharper's Tools: Crooked dice.

Shaver: A risk taker. So called because with the implements of the time a close shave was dangerous indeed close shave has come into common parlance as a dangerous near miss.

Shavings: Coin clippings.

She Napper: One of the few women Thief Takers, a brothel madam or a taker of young virgins.

Shop: Prison.

Shoulder Clapper: Officer of the law.

Shoulder Sham: Accomplice to pick pocket.

Shred: A tailor.

Sice: A Sixpence.

Silent: To knock out.

Silk Snatchers: Thieves of lace.

Simkin: A simpleton or one who pretends to be.

Simon: A Sixpence.

Single Ten: An idiot.

Sir John: A country vicar or Parson.

Skew: Begging bowl.

Skip Jacks: Jockeys who ride horses for sale.

Skipper: A barn.

Skrip: Paper.

Slam: Trick or con.

Slat: A sheet.

Slate: Half Crown: Also a Slot.

Sleeping House: A private house with no cellar and not attached to a shop.

Sly Boots: A guy who seems stupid but is in fact very cunning.

Smacking Cove: A coachman.

Smash: To kick someone down the stairs.

Smear: Painter or plasterer.

Smeller: A nose.

Smelts: Half Guineas.

Smiter: An arm.

Smoky: Suspicious.

Smug: A blacksmith.

Smuggling Ken: A brothel.

Snabble: To plunder, strip or search.

Snaffle: To steal.

Snapt: Caught.

Sneaking Budge: Petty thief who works alone.

Snic: To cut.

Snilch: To spot someone.

Snip: To cheat.

Snite: A blow.

Snudge: Downright weird kind of

housebreaker who hides under a bed until it is quiet enough to rob the place.

Snug: Quiet or the coast is clear.

Sock: Pocket.

Socket Money: Money spent on Marriage.

Soldier's Bottle: A big bottle.

Solomon: Mass.

Son of Apollo: Scholar.

Son of Mars: Soldier.

Son of Venus: A ladies' man.

Son of Mercury: A wit or thief.

Son of Prattlement: A lawyer.

Soul Driver: A parson.

Soul: A brandy lover.

Souse: Penny.

Soudse: To beat cruelly.

South Sea: Contraband alcohol in prison.

South Sea Mountain: Gin.

Sowse Crown: An idiot or one who pretends to be one.

Sow Child: A young girl.

Sowr: To violently beat.

Spanish Gout: Syphilis.

Spanish Money: Compliments.

Spanks: Money or precious metals.

Speckt Wiper: Coloured handkerchief.

Spiritual Flesh Broker: A parson.

Split Fig: A grocer.

Splitter of Causes: A lawyer, specifically a divorce lawyer.

Spring a Partridge: To lure a victim in.

Squab: A fat person also a couch.

Squal: Voice.

Squeek: To cry out, impeach or discover.

Squeeker: Bar boy, bastard or child.

Squeezing of Wax: Under contract or oath or sealing writings.

Squire of Alsatia: A rich man easily parted with his money.

Stag: An enemy.

Stale Jest: Old joke.

Stallion: Pimp.

Stall Whimper: A bastard.

Stammel: A strong lusty prostitute.

Stamps: Legs.

Stampers: Shoes.

Starter: To flinch.

Stick Flams: A pair of gloves.

Stingo: A strong liquor.

Stitch Back: Strong ale.

Stock Drawers: Stockings.

Stone Doublet: A prison.

Stop Hole Abbey: Meeting place of criminals.

Stoter: A fierce hit.

Strapping: A lying prostitute.

Strapping Lass: A woman good at fighting.

Stretching: Hanging.

Stretch: To tell a lie.

Strike: To beg, rob or get oneself in debt.

Strommel: Hair.

Strowlers: General term for Gypsies and wondering performers honest or otherwise.

Strowling Morts: Confidence tricksters who pretend to be widows.

Strum: A wig or a particularly beautiful prostitute or other strumpet.

Stubble It: Hold your tongue.

Suck: Wine or strong drink.

Sucky: Drunk.

Suit and Cloak: Good store of brandy.

Sunburnt: Carrier of Chlamydia.

Sunny Bank: Good winter fire.

Su Pouch: A hostess or landlady.

Sutler: Pickpocket.

Swaddlers: Robbers who delight in violence.

Swag: Shop.

Sweet: Easily taken in or of great roguish skill.

Sweetners: Cheats and con men.

Swinde: To beat soundly.

Tackle: A mistress or fine clothes.

Tale Tellers: In Ireland there was a practice among the gentry for hiring working class "Tale Tellers" to entertain them with the local urban legends.

Talesman: Author.

Tall Boy: A two quart pot.

Tally Men: Corrupt clothes hirers.

Tap: A hit.

Tape: A cocktail of gin, aniseed and clove water.

Taplash: Drunk or speaking rubbish.

Tart Dames: Sharp, quick or pert women.

Tartar: A cheat who betrays or cheats his own kind.

Tatter De Mallion: A raggedy beggar.

Tattle: A look out or watch.

Tats: Rigged dice.

Tayle: Sword.

Tayle Drawers: Sword thieves, particularly dangerous roguish profession.

Teague Land: Ireland.

Tears of the Tankard: Spilt drink.

Temple Pickling: Bribing public officials.

Tender Parnel: A very feeble looking man of substance.

Tercel Gentle: A gentleman up to the rank of Knight.

Thorough Cough: Coughing and farting simultaneously.

Thorough Passage: In one ear and out the other.

Three Legged Stool: Tyburn.

Three Threads: Common ale.

Threpps: Threpence.

Thrums: Threpence.

Thummikins: Use of thumbscrews.

Tib: Young woman.

Tick: To trust.

Tickle Pitcher: A wanker or lewd man or woman.

Tickrum: Licence.

Tiffing: Having sex, drinking or both.

Tilter: Sword. To tilt is to have a sword fight.

Tip: To loan or lend.

Tippler: A wanker.

Tit: A horse or a young pretty girl.

Toge: A coat

Togemans: A Cloak.

Tokens: The plague, presents or a Farthing.

Tol: Sword.

Tom Coney: An idiot.

Tom Thumb: A dwarf or small person.

Tongue Pad: A smooth insinuator.

Tony: An idiot or a whining beggar.

Top Diver: Ladies' man.

Tope: To drink.

Top Heavy: Drunk.

Topping Fellow: A man at the top of his game.

Topping Cheat: The Gallows.

Topping Cove: The hangman.

Tories: Irish thieves. Also the nickname for what would become the Conservative Party.

Totty Headed: Not quite right in the head.

Tour or Tout: To keep your eyes sharp.

Touting Ken: An alehouse or tavern.

Tower Hill Play: Slap in the face and kick in the nuts.

Town Bull: A notoriously promiscuous man.

Tower: Clipped money.

Track: To go, normally with haste.

Transmogrify: To pawn.

Trapan: A lure.

Tres Wins: Threpence.

Trigry Mate: An idle female companion.

Trip: A prison.

Trim: Dress.

Trimming: Conning.

Trine: To hang.

Tripe: The belly.

Trip: As well as the usual modern usage Trip could mean a miscarriage or bastard.

Trooper: Half Crown.

Trull: A prostitute.

Trumpery: Old stuff.

Trunk: Nose.

Trusty Trojan or Trusty Trout: Trusted friend:

Origin of the condom company name.

Tuck'd: Hang'd.

Tumbler: A cart. To shove the tumbler is to be flogged at the cart's tail. Also a trickster or a decoy.

Turk: A cruel hearted man. Yes very racist.

Turkish Shore: Lambeth, Southwark and Rotherhithe.

Turkish Treatment: Bad business.

Turnip Pate: White or very light blonde hair.

Tweak: A rage.

Twelver: Shilling.

Twist: Half tea half coffee, brandy and eggs and to eat generally.

Twisted: Hanged.

Twit: To hit in the teeth.

Unrig'd: Naked or to strip.

Untwisted: Ruined.

Uphills: Dice rigged to roll high.

Uppish: Wealthy and successful.

Upright Men: Gang leaders.

Urchin: Sorry little fellow or destitute child.

Urinal of the Planets: Ireland on account of the fact it rains so much.

Vamp: To pawn.

Vampers: Stockings probably where we get the modern version of vamp from.

Varlets: Servants who have turned to crime.

Vault: To commit acts of debauchery.

Vaulting School: A brothel.

Velvet: A tongue. To tip the velvet is to perform oral sex on a woman.

Vinegar: A cloak and a wrestling or pugilism promoter.

Virago: A woman with masculine traits, usually fighting prowess.

Vouchers: Purveyors of forged money and legal documents.

Waggish: Playful and pleasant. Not like the modern meaning at all!

Wap: To have sex with a man.

Wapper Eyed: Having sore or running eyes.

Warm: A full pocket.

Warming Pan: A large and old fashioned watch. A Scotch Warming Pan is a female bed fellow.

Warren: A man who is security for a loan. Also a

workhouse, new prison or brothel.

Wash: Make up.

Waspish: Peevish.

Water Pad: River based pirate.

Wattles: Ears or folds of sheep.

Web: Cloth.

Wedge: Plate silver or gold small items. Also money.

Wench: A prostitute.

Welsh Fiddle or Scotch Fiddle: Chlamydia.

Westminster Wedding: When a criminal marries a prostitute.

Wet Quaker: A Quaker alcoholic.

Wheadle: A con artist or the con itself.

Whids: Words.

Whiddle: To bribe or to impeach or discover.

Whig Land: Scotland.

Whiners: Prayers.

Whip Shire: Yorkshire.

Whipster: A sharp or subtle man.

Whinyard: A sword.

Whip Jacks: Con artists pulling the old sailor in distress trick.

Whirlegigs: Testicles.

Whiskins: Shallow brown drinking bowls.

Whit: Newgate.

Whitechapel Portion: Two torn smocks and one's natural assets.

White Wool:
Silver.

Whore's Kitling:
Child of a prostitute
or illegitimate child.

Whow Ball: Milk
Maid.

Wibble: To drink
out of sorrow.

Widow's Weeds:
Female morning
clothes.

Winchester Goose:
A prostitute licensed
by the Bishop of
Southwark. The
small certificate
stating "His Grace
the Bishop of
Southwark does
grant me (name)
licence to sin and
take payment." It
has about as much
legal weight as an
IOU but it was a
mark of being a
class above the
common whore in
these deeply
religious times.

Wild Rogues:
Habitual criminals
from a young age
who usually end up
on the business end
of a noose.

Willing Tit: A well
behaved horse or
very friendly
woman.

Willow: Poor and
of no standing.

Win: A Penny. To Win is to steal.

Windy Fellow: A senseless man without reason.

Wipe: A blow.

Wiper: Handkerchief.

Wiper Drawer: Pickpocket or shoplifter who specialises in handkerchiefs.

Wise Man of Gotham: An idiot or someone who pretends to be one.

Witcher: Silver.

Witcher Cully: Silversmith.

Wobble: To boil.

Woman of the Town: A prostitute.

Wooden Ruff: Pillory.

Wood Pecker: One who bets on the success or failure of other gamblers.

In a Wood: In the shit.

Woolly Crown: A simpleton.

Word Pecker: One that is good at playing with words.

Xantippe: Classical reference to Socrates' henpecking wife. Used in general for shrews and henpeckers.

Yam: To eat heartily.

Yarmouth Capon: A red herring.

Yarmouth Coach: Slow vehicle. Usually a shabby cart.

Yarum: Milk or dairy products.

Yea and Nay Men: Quakers or simple folk.

Yellow Boy: A guinea or gold coin.

Yelper: A town crier or one given to lamenting trifling matters.

Yoak'd: Married.

Yorkshire Tike: A Yorkshireman or one who acts like one.

Zad: Crooked.

Zany: A comedy performer of a high class.

Znees: Frost or frozen.

Politics, Society and Religion

And they call this civilisation!

Never Talk about Religion or Politics

BULLSHIT! Sorry but it is. In Britain and many of its former colonies it is considered rude to talk about people's politics, social economic standing and religion.

However there is no better way to work out a person's motivations to look at these key driving factors. Hey that's probably why it's rude… oh well.

Anyhow this section is dedicated to the socio economic structure, political machinations and religious divisions in Georgian society and how you can use these to highlight modern day issues.

The Class System

I have touched upon the Class System in pretty much every single one of the **History Farce** books and it is something that bugs the British to this very day.

There is a good reason for this: It sucks and it is pretty much unchanged since the Restoration. Here is how it works…

Titled Nobility

The vast majority of the movers and shakers in British society were from various inbred "noble" families with the pompous titles to match.

Due to their wealth inherited from their "big murdering bastard" ancestors they control pretty much every key powerbase in the state, church, society and economy.

Of course society is changing and becoming ever more hostile to these old traditions. These fears are well founded in that Cromwell's failed Republic is not long buried and revolution in France breaking out in the late 1700s makes them extremely paranoid of the anarchists under the bed.

They needn't have worried. They're still around today as powerful as ever!

The titled nobility are by and large horribly flawed characters though not necessarily entirely by their own fault.

They are as much victims of the society they lead as the people below them. This is particularly true of the women who are essentially treated as legal sex slaves.

Title Table

This table is in every **History Farce** Game however it is worth repeating as a general reference…

Title	Addressed as
King/Queen	Your Majesty
Princess/Princesses	Your Royal Highness
Duke/Duchess	Your Grace
Marquess	My Lord/ Your Lordship
Marchioness	My Lady/ Your Ladyship
Earl	My Lord/ Your Lordship
Earless	My Lady/ Your Ladyship
Count	My Lord/ Your Lordship
Countess	My Lady/ Your Ladyship
Viscount	My Lord/ Your Lordship
Viscountess	My Lady/ Your Ladyship
Baron	My Lord/ Your Lordship
Baroness	My Lady/ Your Ladyship
Lord of Parliament	My Lord/ Your Lordship
Baronet	Sir
Knight	Sir
Wife of a Knight/ Lord of Parliament (Lady)	My Lady
Member of Parliament	The Right Honourable

Untitled Nobility

Of course the "noble" families are far from the paragons of virtue they claim to be. Thus there are many illegitimate nobles running around without titles from birth (though they are often given them later.)

Untitled nobles fill in most of the gaps in the establishment that aren't filled by their "legitimate" counterparts. Usually this is at the behest of fathers who either have genuine sympathy for them or have had their arms twisted by blackmailing mothers.

Generally untitled nobility have a semi justified chip on their shoulder that is only ever eliminated if they rise above their "legitimate" counterparts which happens once in a blue moon if at all.

The Rising Middle

Ever since Simon DeMontefort established the House of Commons the position of those with no relation to the mafia like "nobility" but with considerable wealth and power nonetheless was firmly established in the British class system.

This middle class are mostly comprised of wealthy large businessmen from the somewhat eccentric industrialists to the shady East India Company agents.

Supporting these is a gaggle of lawyers, accountants and petty bureaucrats who are fast establishing the mess that would become Britain as we know it today.

For as much as the titled and untitled blue bloods would like to deny it, it is not their "breeding" that gives them power it is their money. Increasingly the middle classes are finding themselves with a considerable sum in their grubby hands.

As Orwell observed the middle's central purpose is to push their way up and replace the upper class. In Britain they have come close a couple of times but still no cigar.

Middle class Characters will probably be the 2nd most popular amongst **History Farce** Players after crooks. Especially in **Tough Justice** where they can follow in the footsteps of William

Garrow and fight for their fellow man on the
nobility's playing field.

Skilled Workers

Of the working classes those with the most
respect and standing in society, not to mention
the advantage of cold hard cash were those with
a skill or trade.

Usually learned through an apprenticeship
rather than schooling having a trade allows a
Charter to set up his own business and maybe
even own enough property to get a vote.

Certainly these skilled workers will have the ear
of many rich clients who are so utterly useless
and workshy they would be lost without them,
as much as they refuse to admit it.

I can't see this class being very popular for
Characters but just occasionally it may be fun to
play one. It may sound boring being a humble
cobbler or milliner however it gives you a
position in society that can be extremely useful.

Not to mention that in **Transported** a Trade can be a critical survival skill!

Unskilled Workers

The majority of the population come into the Unskilled Worker category. Any education they do have is rudimentary; indeed the vast majority are likely to be illiterate.

Those that have managed to get some education are likely to be amongst the growing move to unionisation. Though this is highly illegal for the moment it is slowly gaining ground as the toffs figure it's better to have non-violent unionists to negotiate with than a mob dragging a guillotine behind them.

Unskilled Workers make very boring Characters for the most part. They're not particularly canny and tend to be focused entirely on the physical realm.

Having said this as unionisation comes to the fore playing a rather bolshie Baldrick type Character.

Crooks

Crooks aren't necessarily bad people: Economic disparity is such that the vast majority of people are forced to beg, steal, rob and whore to survive.

Thus though it is tempting to play an outright villain there are plenty of wonderful shades of grey within the Georgian Underworld.

The greatest literary heroine of the age Moll Flanders is a classic example of this. When we are introduced to her in Newgate she is apparently a filthy, monstrous animal however as we hear her story we find that in reality she was just a poor girl with pretentions of being a "gentlewoman."

In all of the **History Farce** games Crooks are bound to be very popular: Yes even in **Courtesans**, Upstarts, Actresses and Professionals are rarely the most honest of ladies!

Of course when it comes to criminality **Tough Justice** and **Transported** are obviously the go to games!

Politics

Politics is not a field in which the vast majority of people have any influence whatsoever. Then again it isn't today… because we're British damnit!

The property qualification for voting varies between boroughs but it is usually high enough to keep out the vast majority of the population. Add the sexist qualifier of you having to be male and it gets even worse.

Those who can dabble in the black arts of politics have the following issues to consider…

Parliament

The primary political powerhouse of the nation is Parliament. During the 18th Century it is slowly being divided into the unelected House of Lords and the elected House of Commons.

This process is far from perfect and many of the first Prime Ministers and leading Parliamentarians were in fact titled nobility for not only the 18th Century but much of the 19th Century as well.

In order to become an "honourable member" you need to win a Seat. Each Seat represents an electoral constituency however they have not been changed since the foundation of Parliament under Simon DeMontefort.

Thus, once huge towns that are now just one farmstead have 3 MPs whilst the new city of Liverpool has none at all.

In the former case there is a great deal of room for corruption. Gentlemen could simply purchase the land, become the sole voter and vote themselves into office.

Even if you actually have an electorate there is plenty of room to cheat. Votes are by Hustings where the voters gather and the vote is decided by a show of hands.

I don't think I need to explain to all you crafty toff Players out there how to abuse that situation.

Once safely in a Seat a man gets the title of MP or "Honourable Member." Within Parliament he has the right to speak in the various legislative debates that go on whilst Parliament is in session.

The rules of debate are somewhat lax and open to interpretation by the sitting Speaker though there are two solid rules you cannot break.

1) **Do not cross the line:** There is a line drawn on each side of the House. Members are not to cross this line as it will bring you within swords' length of another Member. Totally not on.

2) **Honourable Members are Honourable:** The worst thing you can do in Parliament is imply a fellow member is not honourable. This means you cannot directly accuse him of lying even if he clearly is. This also means you cannot shake hands in the House. The origin of this friendly gesture was to

affirm neither party was armed with a concealed weapon so it is a massive no-no in the chamber.

The art of circumventing the second rule with creative language is beginning to take shape but will not really become its iconic self until Gladstone and Disraeli in the latter half of the 19th Century.

Another thing that is not fully developed yet is the idea of a political party.

What we have instead are two "proto parties" that would later evolve into fully fledged political entities.

They have no formal names but are instead referred to by their derogatory nicknames.

The Tories

The Tories are a group of landed interest gentry and their cronies concerned with preserving the "moral order and character" of a nation that never really had one.

And people call the various radical elements crazy!

When it comes to legislating the Hell out of everything nobody beats the Tories. They are responsible for the vast majority of the Bloody Code legislation and the use of it to hold the "peasantry" in line.

They are also keen supporters of the establishment of the Church of England (who are known by some as "the Tories at prayer") and the sort of "moral" legislators that the modern world rightly reviles.

Fortunately, for the most part they are held in check by their libertine opponents the Whigs.

The Tories would eventually evolve into the Conservative Party of Great Britain though

1 1 1

many still use the old name derogatorily because, let's face it they're still mostly inherited wealth, tax evading, posh twats!

The Whigs

The Whigs are still, for the most part, landed gentry however they are far more concerned with individual liberty… provided you have the money to enjoy it of course.

Although they are responsible for a lot of the important political progress of the time they only did so for their own personal gain rather than out of actual principle.

Think of them as like the so called "libertarians" of the USA. They talk the talk but really they're all about propping up their own illegitimate position.

Eventually the Whigs would become the Liberal Party which unlike the tightly uniform Conservative Party, was forever fractured into dissenting factions. Some of which eventually got less self-centred!

Radicals

Of course outside of the regular realms of politics are those who actually give a shit about real human beings.

These "Radicals" as they have become known are rarely popular enough with the corrupt system to get themselves Parliamentary Seats (though those that do are in an uneasy alliance with the Whigs) however they campaign in other ways, some of which are less than legal and are liable to get them killed.

Here's a list of a few of the controversial causes of the 18th Century with an assessment of how well their campaigns were.

Catholic Emancipation: A campaign for equal rights under the law for those of the Catholic faith. It had its highs and lows but was eventually successful.

Disestablishtarianism: Got to love that word! This was the campaign to end the privileged status of the Church of England and put all religions on an equal legal footing. It was successful in Ireland as part of the home rule cause and in Wales as part of early Welsh nationalism but in England itself, though Non Conformists and Catholics have better rights the CofE remains the established church.

Home Rule: Britain is not one country it is a collection of countries. Each of these mini countries campaigned long and hard for its independence. Ireland is the most famous of these because it actually won (kind of, see below) but there were also campaigns for Welsh, Scottish and even Cornish home rule.

Unionism: As a reaction to Gladstone's Home rule proposals radical MPs like Lord Randolph Churchill (father of the more famous Winston) started riling up Ireland's Protestant minority claiming "home rule means Rome rule." This was just as incendiary and problematic as Home Rule and with a still divided Ireland we are still suffering the consequences of these shameless opportunists.

Chartism: The Chartists kept up a campaign for universal male suffrage (a few supported women's suffrage but they were in the minority) and proper boundaries for constituencies. It had mixed success. Boundaries were fixed considerably by the two Great Reform Acts but it wouldn't be until 1918 that universal male suffrage finally made law.

Trade Unionism: It was a long hard battle to get Trade Unions recognised in law and there are some days in London where wish they never bothered. Still the Trade Union movement was definitely very undesirable throughout the Demi Monde period. However noble it may have been at this early stage!

Early Socialism: The first people to adopt what we now recognise as socialist ideas were the religious cult known as the Diggers during the Civil War (some say it was the Wyatt rebellion but they miss the very Royalist tone of said failed campaign.) This was just the beginning though. The ideas evolved through the Chartist movement, drew inspiration from the French Revolution and finally adopted the ideas of

1 1 5

obscure German exile Karl Marx as their standard. Like Trade Unionism this was in its early idealistic years before it got any real power and became corrupted.

Abolition of Slavery: A real success story: My ancestor William Wilberforce's campaign to outlaw the slave trade actually worked by the early 1800s. Despite being set back decades by slave rebellions that revisionist historians erroneously give the credit of the abolition to.

Anarchism: From the Chartists and Socialists who wanted better government developed a bunch of extremists who wanted no government at all! Fortunately they didn't get very far.

Women's Rights: A cause your Courtesans can get right behind! By the late 1800s there were two distinct brands of women's rights campaign. The suffragists the peaceful non violent group consisting mainly of the wives and daughters of Liberal MPs and the suffragettes the more militant group who, it is often forgotten, even resorted to outright terrorism at times including an attempted suicide bombing in Dublin! In 1918 it achieved partial success by getting the vote for married women over 30 with a certain amount of property the vote but it wasn't until the 30s that it achieved universal women's suffrage on equal terms with men.

Gay Rights: Believe it or not there were campaigns for the rights of homosexuals even when "sodomy" was a capital crime. Even more surprisingly this was centred in the Church of England and Unitarian and Quaker Churches. Secular campaigners like lesbian landowner Anne Lister also played their part though even they appealed to a sense of Christian justice. It wouldn't be until the 1960s that homosexuality was finally decriminalised though.

Religion

The British people by and large are somewhat liberal and wishy-washy about their religious beliefs.

We have our fanatics of course but the vast majority of the nasty ones fled to America where they were free to persecute people to their heart's content.

Yeah sorry about that, American readers… to quote comedian Hugh Dennis "most of the problems with society overseas are the result of the British Empire messing up and then saying, let's do a runner."

Anyhow despite the rather light hearted attitude of the majority the religious establishment tend to be legalistic and uncompromising.

Everything that Jesus spoke against…

Anyhow let's look at the main religious factions active in the 18th Century.

The Church of England

There is one word to sum up the Church of England: Compromise…

Considering the Church's birth as heavily Catholic Henry VIII's way of getting the divorce the rest of Europe didn't want that was nonetheless run by closet Protestants means it has always been halfway between the Catholic and Protestant positions.

This spirit of one size fits all also applies to attitudes to morality and the mixing of Church and State.

We thus have a Church that is simultaneously supporting and opposing disgusting legislation like the Buggery Act, Slavery and the Death Penalty.

If you think the CofE is divided today it's just two issues that are messing with it. Imagine what it would be like with about half a dozen hot button issues on top of that with just as much debate.

Non-Conformists

Non Conformists are those Protestants who do not accept the authority of the Church of England.

They do not get the same legal benefits as members of the CofE and have to sign the "register of dissent." They are however granted freedom of worship and are not under any particular scrutiny.

Here are a few examples of Non- Conformist Churches.

The Methodist Movement: A young theologian called John Weasley (whose brother Charles wrote the vast majority of popular English Hymns from the era) began a movement within the Church of England to bring Christianity out of the Churches and into the lives of everyday folk. He visited the sick, the poor, the dying and the condemned to die and generally did a very good impersonation of the nice guy version of Jesus. In addition to this "unnecessary enthusiasm" he also didn't seem to give a fig for inter-denominational politics

120

even making use of Greek Orthodox Bishops to ordain more Ministers loyal to the Movement. Thus the Methodists, like pretty much every movement that has tried to stop factionalism and act like ACTUAL Christians since became a denomination of its own that may well be the largest of the Protestant offshoots (as no reliable census can be taken of Christians in China or North Korea this is up for debate.)

Moravians: As the name implies Moravians originate from the central European Kingdom of Moravia however they have been liberally spread throughout Europe for some time. With their rather odd take on ritual and early Protestant ethic against fanciness and indulgences the Moravians were hunted by Catholic establishments and not treated that much better by Protestant ones. Thus they came up with a unique take on Holy Communion which involves sharing a whole meal. When you have to trek to the middle of nowhere to Church breadcrumbs and a sip of wine won't suffice! Anyhow the Moravians are known for being steadfast even in a crisis: In fact especially in a crisis. Though they have this somewhat disturbing enthusiasm they are remarkably open minded and accepting and were the first Church in the UK to ordain a woman as a priest.

Presbyterians: In Scotland and Wales a very different kind of Protestant has the controlling majority. The Presbyterians are far more Protestant than even most of the so called "Low Church" of the CofE. They elect their leaders and have a fashionably dour perspective that has since come to stereotype Scotland in general. When Presbyterians cross the border they find themselves in the unusual position of being a non-conformist like any other though they rarely make a fuss about it.

Unitarians: Another central European import but one that has really taken off in England. Essentially the central tenant of Unitarians is Universal Salvation. Thus they are one of the most open and accepting of all denominations who try their best to get on with everybody. This is thinking some 300 years ahead of everyone else so they tend to be dismissed as a bunch of weirdoes.

Quakers: The Quakers are a home grown liberal Protestant group with similar views to the Unitarians. However they have a very different approach to the issue of liturgy and the concept of Church. Though even the most liberal of other Churches still have a pretty traditional Church layout and a strict order of surface the Quakers depart from this entirely. They are more like a support group than a Church and indeed they prefer their own term "Society of Friends" to Quakers which is more of an informal nickname. Quakers were the first group of Christians in the UK to bless same sex partnerships on an equal basis to marriages.

Baptists/ Pentecostals: You cannot really lump all of these together as each Church is an individual entity with its own policy however they are united enough to count as a denomination in their own right. For the most part they are the very essence of Protestant restraint and minimalism. They are however also associated with the hard-core right of the Church. It is no surprise that the fundamentalist movement that is poisoning Christianity had their origins here. On the upside their missionary work amongst slave populations was a key factor to giving slaves the literacy and courage to fight for themselves rather than rely completely on CofE and Methodist campaigners like William Wilberforce.

Catholics

Though James I tried his damndest to be far more tolerant of Catholicism than his predecessor Elizabeth it was too little too slow and a rather incompetent bunch of wannabe revolutionaries hired a grouchy old mercenary to blow James and Parliament sky high. Their failure means that even over a century later they are the boogeymen of British society.

The days of them being hunted down and killed either within the law or by lynch mob are pretty much over but being an open Catholic gives every bigoted Thief Taker in a mile radius a good reason to pick on you.

As if that wasn't bad enough Catholics are prohibited from holding several key professions and positions of state considered "sensitive" and all Catholic services are confined to private premises.

Yeah welcome to the genuinely persecuted underclass.

Religious Minorities

Britain is slowly becoming a world Empire with the rather fetching pink shade used to denote it fast spreading until it will eventually cover a third of the world's surface.

It is not unheard of not only for the natives of these lands to visit England but also for English people to adopt the religious beliefs of their colonial subjects.

Though few and far between Hindus, Muslims and Buddhists are around in Georgian England and surprisingly they are far better treated than the Catholics when it comes to prejudice and being barred from employment on religious grounds.

One minority that does have a problem however are the Jews. Technically their entire people were exiled back in the 13th Century but the enforcement of this exile was never up to scratch and Jews whether open or covert have played a major role in English life throughout the period where they were technically outlaws.

This does not, however, mean they were treated well. Classical Anti-Semitism coupled with the newer rhetoric of Martin Luther make life hard for England's Jews.

It isn't helped by the fact that their circumstances often force them into petty crime. There is a reason Dickens made his roguish fence Fagin a Jew. It was as common a stupid stereotype as the jive spouting black pimp with a gold cane and purple suit is today and Dickens always loved taking the piss.

Anyhow for the most part a lot of the snobbery of the more exotic faiths was reserved for the upper classes. At the bottom of this crony capitalist nightmare state you tended to have to get along to survive so a little thing like religion was no biggy!

SATANISM !

Not really…

No doubt in a society dominated by repressive Christian social engineering there were pockets of people who did actually worship the other guy because the stuff he was in favour of sounded awesome.

However the most famous "satanic" group of the era: The Hellfire Club were basically engaging in an early form of trolling.

They were a group of very wealthy "gentlemen" who were a mixture of atheists, agnostics and very liberal Christians who met for massive drunken debauched parties and "rituals" that mocked the conventional religious sensibilities of the time.

Registered members included several American Founding Fathers and the father of modern Capitalism Adam Smith. Remember that the next time some idiot teabagger goes on about America being a "Christian Country."

Later on in the Victorian era there was a brief Occult/ Spiritualist craze that led to the works of Crowley and his successors who took the idea of Satanic worship way more seriously than the old trolls of the Hellfire Club.

Extreme and odd Christian cults such as the Plymouth Brethren are around and horribly mistrusted by the people but the government remains too lazy to act.

Key Events and People

Some Landmark Moments and Characters in the 18th Century

I hate Dates

Yeah both kinds but that is another story.

One of the reasons I'm not an academic is because as good a memory I have for quotes and the basic shape of events I'm hopeless with precise dates.

However there are some very important events in the period that those who want to mess around with **History Farce** games ought to know. These momentous events can make a great starting point for a game or can happen in the background to frame the events of the story.

Games Master (of any variety) or Player (of any variety) these events provide a wealth of Character inspiration and can influence the background of anyone from the lowliest to the most exalted.

Be prepared for highs, lows and what the Hells: Often in the same event!

The Death of Queen Anne

The Death of Queen Anne, the last of the Stuart Dynasty, in 1714 was both the beginning of the Georgian age and a terrible blow to the British emotional consciousness.

Anne didn't really do very much but drink and put on a happy face as she buried 10 of her children however that did not stop the rather silly and odd masses from wailing in the streets!

I suppose it was a fair reaction in hindsight as in the next 56 years England would have two Kings who couldn't even speak English but that doesn't make Anne any less useless.

A law was passed commanding all court Officials to wear black gowns and white wigs in mourning. That law has never been repealed so even some 300 years later lawyers still dress this way in the High Court.

You know traditions are nice and all but it does get silly when your justice system is still showing respect for a useless old bat almost 3 centuries dead!

The Publication of Moll Flanders

Daniel Defoe's second novel **"The Fortunes and Misfortunes of Moll Flanders"** in 1721 was quite controversial to say the least.

Its heroine is set up from the outset to be everything its target audience despised. Born to a thieving whore in Newgate, raised by gypsies, Married 5 times, often bigamously, once to her own brother and to top it all sentenced to death for theft. However in telling her story Defoe shows the unfortunate innocent beneath all this seemingly monstrous "immorality" and creates a sympathetic character that the reader can certainly root for.

Of course when a book full of sex, violence and anything resembling reality comes out some dizzy drip is going to want to ban it. Unlike the later and more explicit **Fanny Hill** however they completely failed.

The controversy however stuck and unfortunately the book was more popular as legal porn than as the social political work it was meant to be.

Sophia Baddeley (1745-1786)

Sophia Baddeley followed in the footsteps of Nell Gwyn taking both dramatic and comic roles on the London stage to rave reviews. Of course it was not her acting talent that interested the great and the good.

Escaping an abusive marriage to her director she set herself up as a Courtesan. She was kept mistress to a considerable number of influential people.

If she had one weakness however it was in the management of her money. She reputedly turned down one suitor's very generous Keeping Contract saying that it would not even pay for her milliner.

This combined with several near fatal overdoses on Laudanum sent her on a terrible slide into debt and depression.

133

However unlike many of her peers she had the good fortune of a fan-base that cared enough to set up a fund for her upkeep.

She spent her last years on a small stage in Scotland before she was laid to rest beneath a modest but nonetheless prominent headstone.

Her Companion (and rumoured lover) Eliza Steel also pioneered the tell-all memoir albeit on her "dearest love's" behalf. This was a pattern taken up by later Courtesans including Harriette Wilson who was infamous for charging former lovers for their anonymity: Narrowly skirting the blackmail laws.

Sophia Baddeley was far more than just a Courtesan. She was a successful career woman and high society darling. It is a crying shame that her inability to manage her money and the sheer emotional pressure of several overbearing men brought her to an early death.

Well at least one person loved her...

Elizabeth Armistead (1750-1842)

A Courtesan in the "Professional" mode Armistead was something of a polar opposite of Baddeley in her very careful and restrained money and indeed life management. She's also interesting in that she "redeemed" herself by marrying one of her favourite lovers.

The story of her courtship and marriage to the notorious Radical Whig ringleader Charles Edward Fox (ancestor of the famous acting dynasty) was the greatest love story of the 18th Century and unlike most of its competitors was probably actually genuine.

Her happy ending as respected statesman's widow is something for **Courtesans** players to aspire to: Though they will probably fail!

The American War of Independence

This little spat with the biggest of Britain's colonies had quite an impact on the mother country too.

First a little myth busting: The British did not raise taxes they reduced them and the local smuggling community didn't like loss of income so they manipulated the local hired help to start the Boston Tea Party.

So the stupid led by rich devious criminals... not just the history of America but the history of the world!

Anyhow that's beside the point. The American War of Independence was by far the most important conflict that Britain was involved in during the 18th Century. The short lived Jacobite rebellions were valiant efforts but in the end completely in vain.

America's successful break from the Empire was a humbling blow to the nation as a whole.

Britain was no longer invincible… the lion had been held back from a prey that, though they were armed and supported by the French should have been a pushover on paper.

A lot of very disheartened and sometimes deranged soldiers from all social classes are back in society once the dust has settled. The strain this puts on both individuals and wider society leads to the kind of events that would doubtless be a good basis for the shenanigans of a good **History Farce** game.

Players of **Transported** should also note that the loss of America moves penal colonies to Australia.

Needless to say my sample stories rely heavily upon this event which tears into my "metaplot" like a ravenous wolf!

William Garrow (1760-1840)

A key figure familiar to **Tough Justice** Players from his call to the Bar in 1783 William Garrow was a trailblazer for the rights of the defendant and had a considerable impact on developing the British Criminal Justice system beyond the atrocious state it was when he began his career.

Whether Defending or Prosecuting Garrow's zeal for the truth and some measure of justice in a world of presuppositions, prejudices and rampant corruption is a shining example of what a lawyer should be then and now.

Just to put Garrow's principles into perspective the blatantly corrupt Thief Taker system was one of his first targets and through his pressure England was slowly moving toward a professional Police Force with the County of Middlesex's Bow Street Runners. However when said Bow Street Runners turned out to similarly corrupt he had no qualms about calling out the organisation that was more or less what he proposed when he took on the corruption of the Thief Takers.

Garrow's story is even more remarkable considering his humble origins. He was not Public Schoolboy he was in fact simply apprenticed to an Attorney.

For him to get to High Court Judge, the aid of the radicals and his aristocratic wife not withstanding from such an inauspicious position is somewhat unique though History Farce games being fiction and Player Characters being naturally awesome you're welcome to try to follow a similar trajectory.

The Madness of King George

George III was never quite right in the head but hey he's part of a long line of inbred idiots so nobody noticed really.

The loss of America however, seemed to make something snap.

The massively inbred crown families of Europe are pretty much all afflicted with the hereditary disease Porphyria. One of the most pronounced symptoms of this is susceptibility to psychosis (yeah... great for lifelong heads of state) and with all the stress George had put himself under he went from mildly eccentric to full blown psychotic.

In 1794 he was declared unfit to rule and his son (who wasn't much saner by most accounts) was declared Prince Regent.

This Regency is often romanticised and celebrated and for the most part this is somewhat misplaced. If there was a change, which is somewhat unlikely it had nothing to do with the original Georgie Porgy.

Yes seriously that's the origin of the nursery rhyme. So neo Victorian parents of the world the next time you hear your sweet little munchkin chanting that rhyme do remember what they are talking about is an obese, inbred, lecher chasing after young girls half his age because he was the de-facto King at the time!

Joking aside this was the most public failure in the Monarchy to the date. As much as the establishment tried to hide this "divinely appointed leader" was in fact a complete psychotic they really didn't have a hold on it.

Emerging Newsprint like **The Times** (which back then had the same tone and reputation as the modern tabloids) got the details and ran with them talking of how George was wondering round the palace in his nightshirt talking to plants.

Royal approval would never be the same again though unfortunately they're not done for yet.

Anne Lister (1791-1840)

When it comes to the treatment of homosexuals in Georgian England the key factors were politics and wealth. Anne Lister was fortunate to be born an heiress in a remarkably tolerant community in Yorkshire and thus escaped the legal and social persecution many of her inclination suffered.

In an age where men and women of little wealth or social support were being hanged for their "sodomy" Lister was incredibly open though precise details of her active love life would not be beyond rumour and innuendo until the decryption of her diaries in the 20th Century.

She named 3 lovers the third of which Ann Walker she "married" in 1834. Ann was also an heiress whom Ann had been in business with in her work with local industrialists. They frequently took excursions to Europe where… sadly in 1840 Anne took ill and died in her wife's arms.

Anne is credited as the "first modern lesbian" and is credited with paving the way for many lesbian women to come out of the closet in subsequent years.

Including a wife of an Archbishop of Canterbury but that's another story for another time.

Sexuality comes up in **Doxy** and **Courtesans** of course but it can also be an interesting theme in **Tough Justice** and **Transported** as well.

Though homophobia here in Britain is more muted and subtle than in the USA it is still an issue that I believe the usually very tolerant and accepting gaming community should address.

Final Word

I shall keep this brief… Something very difficult for me to do but I shall try my best.

The Georgian era is… thank God… over but its mentality and crazed hypocrisy is very present in today's world.

Most readers of this book are just after a little primer for their silly romps through the age of silk stockings and hemp nooses but let us never forget that the 18th Century happened and from the attitudes of some rhetoricians could easily happen again unless we remain vigilant.

As always, while writing this, I have a terrible feeling I am far, far too late.

Ian Warner

Directing Editor
Kittiwake Classics

Kittiwake Classics
Contact Details

Blog: http://kittiwake.blog.co.uk
PDF Store:
http://www.rpgnow.com/index.php?manufacturers_id=4009&affiliate_id=151700
Lulu Store:
http://www.lulu.com/spotlight/Kittiwake_Classics
Facebook Page:
http://www.facebook.com/KittiwakeClassics

Directing Editor's Details
YouTube:
http://www.youtube.com/user/DarthAzabrush
Email: darth_azabrush@hotmail.co.uk
Facebook: http://www.facebook.com/i.s.warner

6824217R00082

Printed in Great Britain
by Amazon.co.uk, Ltd.,
Marston Gate.